# The Buzz About Honeybees

By Emily Costello

CELEBRATION PRESS
Pearson Learning Group

# Contents

Introduction . . . . . . . . . . . . . . . . . 3

The Parts of a Honeybee . . . . . . . 6

Types of Honeybees . . . . . . . . . 9

How Honeybees Talk . . . . . . . . 14

Keeping Honeybees . . . . . . . . . 17

Bees in the United States . . . . 21

Glossary . . . . . . . . . . . . . . . . . 24

Index . . . . . . . . Inside Back Cover

# Introduction

Bees have been flying on Earth for millions of years. Though some people fear bees, they are very useful insects.

Bees help fruits and vegetables to grow. This happens as the bees collect **nectar** and **pollen** from flowers for food.

This bee fossil is 35 million years old.

Without bees, we'd have fewer fruits and vegetables to eat. The bees shown are gathering pollen from flowers of a broccoli plant, an apple tree, and an apricot tree.

When a bee moves to a new flower, pollen brushes off its hairy body. The pollen helps the flower to begin making seeds or fruit.

All bees, from fuzzy bumblebees to honeybees, spread pollen. However, of all the thousands of types of bees, only honeybees make large amounts of honey.

People have been eating honey made by honeybees for a long time. In fact, honey has been found in the tombs of Egyptian kings who lived thousands of years ago. The honey could still be eaten!

In this book, you will learn how honeybees live and act. You'll even meet a young **beekeeper**.

# The Parts of a Honeybee

The most feared part of a honeybee is its stinger. Bee stings are painful. However, honeybees only sting to protect themselves or their **hive**. In fact, most of them die after stinging. The bees leave their stingers behind in a person's or animal's skin.

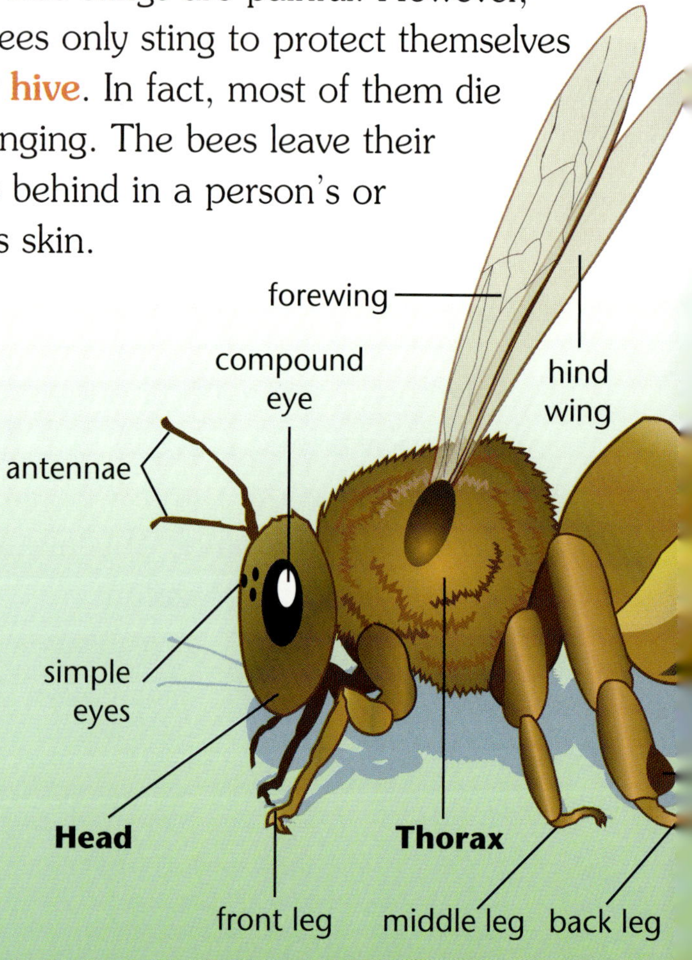

- forewing
- compound eye
- hind wing
- antennae
- simple eyes
- **Head**
- **Thorax**
- front leg
- middle leg
- back leg

Like all insects, a honeybee has a body with three sections: the head, **thorax**, and **abdomen**. Honeybees' bodies are covered with hairs. Pollen sticks to them.

Honeybees have *five* eyes! Two large eyes on each side of the head, called compound eyes, sense movement. On top of the head are three simple eyes that see light and dark.

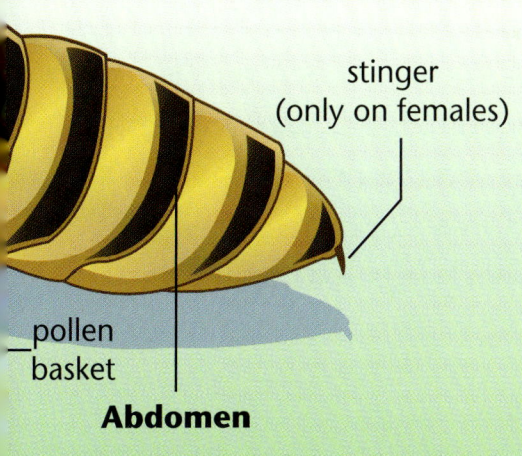

stinger
(only on females)

pollen basket

**Abdomen**

7

The worker bee carries pollen in its pollen baskets.

Honeybees have six legs. Each pair is different. The bee sometimes uses the front pair to clean its **antennae** and the middle pair to walk. On some honeybees, called worker bees, the back legs have special baskets for carrying pollen back to the hive.

# Types of Honeybees

There are three types of honeybees: queens, worker bees, and drones. Thousands of honeybees live together in a hive. Each bee has a different job to do.

Only one queen lives in a hive. It is the largest bee in the hive. The other bees feed and **groom** it. The queen works hard, too. It can lay more than two thousand eggs every single day! A queen bee usually lives for about two or three years.

Most of the bees in a hive are worker bees. All worker bees are female. They clean the hive, feed the queen, collect nectar, and do much more. Worker bees born in the summer live about six weeks. In other seasons, when they are less active, they can live for several months.

The males in the hive are called drones. There are usually only a few hundred in a hive. Drones don't have pollen baskets or a stinger. Yet, they are important. They mate with the queen. Drones live from a few weeks to a few months. Worker bees drag them out of the hive when the weather turns cool.

Honeybees tending larvae in cells near their queen.

All three types of honeybees go through four stages of life. The stages are egg, larva, pupa, and adult.

Bees make a **comb** from wax, which comes out of their abdomen. The queen lays her eggs in the hive's comb. Bee eggs are not much bigger than a grain of sand.

A honeybee starts to grow right after the queen lays the egg. After three days, each egg hatches into a larva. This young form of the bee has no wings.

In just five days, the larva grows to more than 1,500 times its original size. After nearly a week, worker bees seal each larva into its cell with wax.

The larva spins a cocoon of silk around its body. The cocoon is like a house that protects the larvae. Then, the wormlike larva becomes a pupa. During this time its eyes, legs, and wings take shape. Its body turns yellow and black. Fine hairs grow all over its body.

After 12 days, if the pupa is a worker bee, it finally chews its way out of the cocoon and the wax cap. Drones take a few more days to grow than worker bees. Queens take a few days less.

These pupae will develop into African honeybees.

A newborn worker bee's first jobs are in the hive. It cleans cells, feeds larvae, makes wax, and fans its wings to keep the hive cool. It also guards the hive.

When a worker bee is about 22 days old, it becomes a field bee. Now it flies out of the hive. Its job is to gather pollen, nectar, and water.

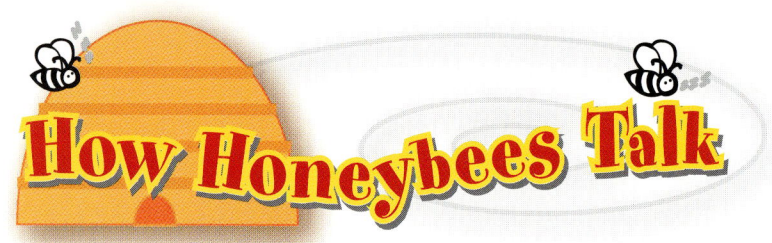

# How Honeybees Talk

Honeybees often have important things to tell other bees. A bee that has found flowers may need help collecting the food. Also, a bee guarding the hive must warn the others if a bear or other animal should attack.

This bee is doing the round dance.

One way honeybees talk to each other is by dancing inside the hive. Worker bees do two main types of dances, the round dance and the waggle dance. The round dance tells other worker bees that food can be found near the hive. A bee doing a round dance moves in a circle. It goes in one direction first, then the other.

This bee is doing the waggle dance for other bees.

The waggle dance tells the worker bees where to find food that is far from the hive. A worker bee doing the waggle dance wiggles its abdomen from side to side while moving in a pattern like a figure eight. The dancing bee's speed tells the other bees how far away the food is. Its movements tell the other bees in what direction to fly. Other bees can also smell the kind of food that the dancer has found.

Honeybees also tell one another things by giving off odors, or smells. Members of a hive have an odor that helps them to recognize one another. Worker bees also release an alarm odor. It lets other bees know they should come to help the hive. The queen produces a "queen substance." This smell tells the other bees that the queen is there. If the queen dies, the hive knows because this smell goes away.

# Keeping Honeybees

People keep honeybees for different reasons. Some beekeepers like to study bee life. Others keep the bees because they want to earn money by selling the honey and **beeswax**. Many people in the United States keep honeybees.

Some people keep beehives in their yards.

Beekeepers who keep honeybees for the honey need to be able to get the honey out of the beehives. Beekeepers can remove the honey by smoking the bees. Beekeepers use smokers to puff cool, white smoke in and around the hive. The smoke calms the bees. Then the beekeepers are able to remove the honey.

Beekeepers use smokers to quiet the hive.

Seth Butcher helps his grandfather keep bees.

Seth Butcher lives in Illinois. Seth's grandfather is a beekeeper. He has been teaching Seth about beekeeping. Sometimes Seth helps his grandfather with his beehives. Seth thinks working with the bees is exciting.

Seth was asked about beekeeping in an interview. Here is what Seth had to say about working with bees.

**Q:** What do you do to help your grandfather with his beehives?

**A:** I smoke the bees to get them out of the hive, and this quiets them down. Then I sometimes hold the frames that have over a hundred bees crawling on them.

**Q:** What part of beekeeping is the most interesting?

**A:** Probably taking out the frames and looking at all of the bees. I look for drones usually because I like to hold them, as they do not have stingers.

**Q:** What is your favorite part about beekeeping?

**A:** Looking for different types of bees when the hive is open. Smoking them is cool, too.

# Bees in the United States

About 4,000 kinds of bees are **native** to the United States. These include bumblebees, digger bees, and others.

Honeybees, however, are not native to the United States. People brought honeybees to the United States from Europe in about 1622. These people made money by selling the bees' honey. They also made candles from beeswax.

Some of the bees escaped from their hives. They became wild. Soon they were everywhere.

One kind of honeybee that now lives in the United States is known as the "killer bee." "Killer bee" is a nickname for the Africanized honeybee. Where did these killer bees come from?

In the 1950s scientists brought African honeybees to Brazil to study. Some bees got loose by accident. They mated with other bees. A new mix of bees, Africanized bees, began to spread north.

About 40 years later these bees reached America. They are more likely than other honeybees to **swarm**.

Killer bees came to the United States from South America.

Africanized honeybees look like other honeybees.

A person could be stung by many of these bees at once. Although the bees only sting in defense, some animals and a few people have died from their stings.

Honeybees should not be disturbed when they're doing their important work. After all, these fuzzy little bees just might be the most useful insects on earth.

# Glossary

**abdomen** — the back part of a bee's body that holds some of the bee's organs

**antennae** — feelers found on an insect's head

**beekeeper** — a person who raises bees

**beeswax** — a substance that honeybees release, which is used in making candles, polishes, and other things

**comb** — a structure made of wax cells by bees to hold food and their eggs

**groom** — to make neat and clean

**hive** — a home for bees

**native** — living or growing naturally in a particular place

**nectar** — the sweet, watery liquid made by plants

**pollen** — a powdery substance made by flowers

**swarm** — to gather and fly off in large numbers

**thorax** — the middle part of a bee's body where the legs and wings are attached